*You cannot let the weight
of this world obscure
the light that you
carry within.*

Praise for the prayers of Lyna Rose

"Lyna Rose has a lovely voice, soft and tender but deep and serious. I harken to the sound of her prayers."
— MARIANNE WILLIAMSON

"In a world of spiritual self-help books, it's a thrill of the soul to come upon *Enlighten Your Life*, a gift of impeccable teaching that can guide you to your own indispensable truth. I feel as though I've stumbled upon the journals of a saint, the electricity of one who has tussled to ignite her light, and who writes like a dream, yet a human being I can relate to, one who fills my bones with courage, love and recognition. This book is sweetness, strength, and genius."
— TAMA KIEVES, USA TODAY-featured visionary career catalyst and best-selling author of *A Year without Fear: 365 Days of Magnificence and Thriving through Uncertainty*

"For those who work with *A Course in Miracles*, I heartily recommend this trenchant book of ACIM-inspired prayers by Lyna Rose. Lyna's brief preface on the hype and reality of prayer is itself a statement that you will never forget." — MITCH HOROWITZ, author of *One Simple Idea: How Positive Thinking Reshaped Modern Life*

"Lyna Rose's magic is that she's able to transmute our mistakes and problems into exquisite and uncommon states of grace. She takes us on a journey that starts between a rock and a hard place, and ends in a subtle state of peace and joy. Readers will enjoy this book for other reasons, too. For one, Lyna's personal revelations keep the reader continuously engaged in what she's saying. She also takes the time to be original, presenting her ideas in fresh, compelling ways. Best and last, Lyna brings extraordinary writing talent and beauty into her work, and this is a great pleasure for the reader."
— KAREN BENTLEY, best-selling author of *The Power to Stop: stopping as a path to self-love, personal power and enlightenment*

"A beautiful and touching collection that speaks to the needs of many today. It gives a whole new freshness and depth to prayer." — RICHARD SMOLEY, author of *The Deal: A Guide to Radical and Complete Forgiveness*

"What I love about Lyna's prayers and meditations is that she touches on so many subjects and reveals her own struggles. You can dip into this book again and again, and always come away with new inspirations about anything that's challenging you. And she's just a beautiful writer." — REV. MARIA FELIPE, author of *Live Your Happy: Get Out of Your Own Way to Discover the Love Within*

"The gentle beauty of this book will help you realize the light within you. I love the way Lyna captures the important principle of taking full responsibility for our state of mind, yet lovingly helps guide us to bring our fears and uncertainties to the Truth of our oneness. These inspired prayers will return the mind to a condition of peace." — CINDY LORA-RENARD, author of *A Course in Health and Well-Being*, international speaker on *A Course in Miracles*, and Spiritual Life Coach

Enlighten Your Life

52 PRAYERS
with VISUALIZATIONS, AFFIRMATIONS & LOVE

Grace & love

LYNA ROSE

FEARLESS BOOKS

SONOMA · CA

FEARLESS BOOKS
info@fearlessbooks.com

ISBN: 978-0-692-06750-5

PHOTOGRAPHY:
Olivia Cano Graff

DESIGN & TYPOGRAPHY:
D. Patrick Miller

TABLE OF CONTENTS

FOREWORD

W HAT A delightful, honest, meaningful, and well-written series of prayers and meditations!

I got to know Lyna Rose as a student in my classes on *A Course in Miracles* in New York City, and she remains a true friend. Lyna's absentee mother was severely alcoholic, and her father remains unknown. Her first husband left her days after her first daughter was born. Out of necessity Lyna has learned how to pray — progressing from asking for a real father and mother as a child, to communing with her spiritual Father as an adult.

Sometimes life puts us through incredible trials, and some folks crumble under the weight of life and all its responsibilities. Yet if we pay attention and pray in all sincerity, something deep within can lift us up and help us through life's bitter tests.

Ardent in prayer and ever seeking — moving ever more profoundly into loving God — Lyna's hardships have led her to see that prayer and communion are the same. Like so many seekers, Lyna has had to learn her way through the tragedies of life. Prayer has led her deeper and deeper into an exploration of the inner life, and an awareness that the 'Kingdom of Heaven' lies only within, and that answers to the deeper questions of life are never found in the world. What Lyna has learned is that prayer means observing without judgment, interpretation, or analysis.

Her lessons have come in learning to forgive over and again.

Prayer is the recognition that the same Love that many see in Jesus is in the Universe at large, and thus also in us all. It just needs to be uncovered and expressed.

As we give our lives away in love, love comes our way and so do the answers to our prayers — perhaps not in the form we expected, but always telling us that God is with us, no matter how severe our trials.

Prayer is a state of communion and a direct awareness of God as the ground of our being. As Lyna puts it, the answer to prayer comes "in renouncing the wishes that do not serve our highest good." Once such wishes can be put aside, then God is at liberty to answer the true prayers of our heart.

— JON MUNDY, PH.D., publisher of *Miracles Magazine*, and author of *Living A Course in Miracles*

INTRODUCTION

"PRAYER is the medium of miracles," reveals the spiritual teaching known as *A Course in Miracles*. "It is a means of communication of the created with the Creator. Through prayer love is received, and through miracles love is expressed."

When I first prayed on my own as a little girl, in the musty corner of my bedroom in Normandy, France, I asked God for a real father and a real mother. My mother had been absent for several months and my great-grandparents, my childhood caretakers, did not know her whereabouts. I didn't know who my father was.

I prayed through tears that God would change my mother into a normal, doting mother. But her chronic alcoholism and absence only grew.

In fact, I never seemed to get my prayers answered during the first part of my life. I would always ask for my life to change, but most times it just went from bad to worse.

After my great-grandparents passed, I remember praying for a different foster family after a few years of disparagement and emotional abuse. Yet my second foster family only sharpened my sense of being a wretched creation, condemned to walk in the shoes of my mother. Later I prayed for my American boyfriend to love me, and instead he divorced me one month after I gave birth to my first daughter.

God did not transform my mother because she didn't need to be fixed — she only needed to be loved. What God did do for me was to offer a perfect path of trenches, hurdles, and open space that would eventually mold my heart into a chamber of forgiveness and compassion.

Prayer does not exist so that we may get our way, and God is not Santa Claus. Prayer exists so that we may align our mind and our heart with the divine order of happiness that exists deep within us, but is so often forgotten. Prayer is the sacred, energetic path to our inner life, the lifeline of our holiness. It is a noble stairway to a greater consciousness, so that we can learn to undo our resistance to life and love.

When I pray, I do it in order to step out of the way of the divine. I may still want things to change, but I understand that I'm not in charge of change. I'm not asking for favors from God. Instead of seeking correction of whatever may seem to be going wrong, I pray to be molded into the highest realization of my Self.

Prayer enables us to disengage from fear-driven thinking; it is a silken cloth that wipes away our heart's anxieties. I offer the following prayers, along with some related visualizations and affirmations, to help you release your fears, know the divine energy of love within you, and realize your ultimate happiness. They are written in a first-person voice not just because they began with my own experience, but because I want them to become your experience as well. Please use the ones you can, and repeat or adapt them as you wish. Eight of the prayers are offered as short Meditations that address the state of mind of praying itself.

I have tried to think of enough life circumstances, challenges, and opportunities to last you for at least a year of inspiration. But I hope that courage, love, and divine creativity are with you always. These words are the result of what I have learned about prayer so far, but now they are yours to practice and evolve for your own purposes. — *Lyna Rose*

Twelve Ways to Look at Prayer

PRAYER IS:

A trail of divine love within us

A loving filter for our consciousness

The offering of our will unto life itself

A sacred command over our perception

An echo of the Universe tailored to our true needs

The attunement of our thoughts with the laws of creation

The scaffolding of our budding intimacy with the Divine

The surrender of fear in favor of persistent gratitude

A transformative exchange between all our selves

The remembrance of love's presence within us

The agreement to accept our holiest good

An invitation to the breath of life
to enter and heal our darkest wounds

MEDITATION I:
Clearing the Past

I am the sole master of my existence
and I do not have to fall into
a repetition of the past.
Tenderly I erase the effects of my history
from the screen of my mind, and
let today's reality be free of darkness.
My past is now just a story
safely stored within my heart,
and I feel the dance of life
leading me into joy.

PRAYERS FOR
Relationships

*Look at your heart
as the source of everything
you want to experience in this life.*

Prayer to Overcome
Resistance to Romance

Dear Healer of the Universe,
I despair that I will never meet the love I hope for.
All my past romantic pursuits have failed.
I feel that I am too damaged for love
and I have decided not to need a partner.

Perhaps I am not meant to be with someone;
maybe I am meant to spend the rest of my life alone.
I feel cursed by love.

Guide me to remove this
debilitating resistance from my heart.
Help me see that I am the one
creating barriers against romance.
Help me to allow all my disappointments and fears
to be seen and transformed so that they may
nurture my soul back to wholeness.

Let me be grateful for all the lessons
of past heartbreaks because they can lead me
to a wholesome understanding
of my heart's true desires.
Bless me with sacred cognizance
of my inner and outer beauty.
Amen.

VISUALIZATION

See with your inner vision your heart floating in the open air right in front of you. Feel a faraway wind rushing toward you, as you yearn to be cleansed from past fears that have kept your heart tucked away. As the wind arrives with its swift power and reverent love, it cascades over your heart and sweeps away the remnants of mistrust, doubt, and betrayal that have kept it so guarded. As you place your hands over your heart space now, know that your old defenses have gone with the wind, and you can feel at peace and at ease with yourself.

AFFIRMATIONS

I trust the inner desires of my heart.
I am willing to let love in.
I am loveable even when I am afraid.
I release my resistance to let love come to me.

Prayer for
Surrender in Romance

Dear God,
I have made someone special,
and feel that I need this person to love me
for me to feel good enough about myself.

I want to be loved in a way that eases
my fears and my deepest insecurities.

I am willing to melt in union
with you, dear God, so that I may not turn to
a special person for completion and happiness.

Help me be free of the thoughts that attach
my well-being to another's behavior.

Gently guide my heart to its throne
of mastery over ancient fears.

Heal my projections
of abandonment so that my heart
may open itself fully to the present time.

I place my attachment into your all-knowing hands
so that my surrender may bless us both
with an increased awareness of love.
Amen.

Visualization

Visualize your beloved standing in front of you in the space overlooking the Earth. As you embrace one another, your respective inner lights gradually grow in brightness, and extend beyond you until you are surrounded by a brilliant cocoon. Your respective beauty and strength become magnified through your union bathed in light. Now visualize your beloved moving farther and farther away, until no longer visible to your outer eyes. Yet the love you share still joins you. Your beloved has gone into the faraway depths of the Universe, escaping all toxic attachments. Only love is left inside of you now.

Affirmations

I release all expectations about romance, giving this relationship to a higher power for transformation.

I choose to focus on the love in my heart.

I revel in my own divinity.

The beauty and strength of my beloved reflect the holiness already dwelling within me.

Prayer to Reconnect
With a Partner

Dear Beloved God,
I no longer feel connected to my partner
and I haven't felt truly seen in a long time.
Our hearts are disconnected and
our bodies are no longer in tune.

I am anxious that the young lovers we once were
no longer breathe into each other's heart.
Brighten the path back to each other.
Melt the militant walls around my heart
to let my vulnerability flow into my partner's heart.

May I demonstrate
unconditional acceptance for both of us.
May I let go of my agenda
so that I can focus on
our unseen potential together.

Scrape our cobbled past from my perception
so that I may see us truly once again.
May I lead with my heart even when my rejected ego
wants to run away to protect itself.

As I lean toward our joined hearts again,
may I create a greater bond with the heart of my lover.
Amen.

VISUALIZATION

Place your hands upon your heart and visualize a bright white light dancing around it. Now gently ask that healing light to melt all your fearful defenses, knowing it is safe to let love in. Ask your heart its deepest fears and its greatest hopes. Allow your inner voice to guide you, and do not judge any guidance that will arise. What is the imaginary pain your heart is protecting you from? What is your secret dream for this romance? When you allow yourself to connect with your heart and accept what it desires, you open up the connection with other hearts as well. As your heart becomes wide open and charged with unconditional love, you are now willing to let yourself be vulnerable and authentic. There is no risk because your own soul will support and nurture you. See the light of your heart opening merging with your partner's heart and connect to how great it feels to be at one again.

AFFIRMATIONS

I breathe unconditional love into the pain that distances me
from my partner.
As I become more open, my heart becomes a magnet.
I nurture myself emotionally so that I can partner without need.
My partner and I are one in heart.

Prayer to Release
A Partner

Dear Love,
My heart is invaded by
the shadows of a past relationship.
Although years have passed, this lover's spirit
still lingers at the edges of my mind.
I have not yet let go of the fantasy
of finding this special one again
and that illusion is locking my heart.

I feel blocked from the universal love
that would enable my growth.

I am willing, at last,
to let go of my grip on the past.
Please cleanse me from the old energies
of our relationship and our triggered wounds.
May the places we carved in each other be blessed
and healed in our memories forever.

I release this special person back to you.
Farewell, dear lover.
Amen.

VISUALIZATION

Welcome into your mind the past partner that remains attached to your heart. Now see his or her face right in front of you. You are facing each other, sitting in a cross-legged position. Close your eyes to center your focus on your inner world, and the emotions arising from being in each other's presence. Those emotions are welcome for whatever they are. They are free to be. Let yourself dwell in the immensity you feel for that partner. No emotion is wrong.

Now you notice a red energetic cord joining both of you, floating from the center of your being to your partner's heart. Become willing to cut that profound bond so that you may both continue on your individual paths. Say to yourself: "I am willing to let go." See a curtain of light forming between the two of you, cutting the red cord, jolting you both momentarily. Let out the tears that want to leave your body as you are now a little lighter and freer, and silently thank your ex-partner for the love you shared.

AFFIRMATIONS

My heart knows how to heal itself. I can trust its guidance.
I forgive myself for what I couldn't bring to this relationship.
I feel the joy of new possibilities.
I am grateful for the miraculous growth offered by my relationship.

Prayer to Guide a Breakup

Dear Life,
I am caught in a whirlwind of confusion
regarding my current relationship.
I feel disconnected from love
and do not feel adequately embraced.
I cannot seem to release my ego's needs
to be fed by the heart of another
instead of the steady nurturance
of my own soul.

Grace me with the courage to act
and honor my true heart above all else.

May the rest of our relationship run its holiest course,
be it in friendship or renewed romance.
Remind me not to project the gloomy veil
of my past wounds onto my partner.
Grant me the emotional dexterity
to fill my own unmet needs
and thus see the situation clearly.
And so it is,
AMEN.

Visualization

Invite your imagination to open up to all the possibilities of your being. Now visualize yourself doing exactly what you want to be doing in your wildest dreams...being exactly who you want to be. Where are you? What are the colors of the room? What are you wearing?

Now in the background of that situation, see someone standing and watching you, with pride to be your partner and enormous love vibrating from their heart towards you. You feel empowered and supported by this person's love and pride. This is the partner you are meant to have. The timing will be perfect, as a power greater and wiser than yourself will orchestrate the meeting and guide the relationship. Dwell in the feelings of that vision and keep it tucked in your heart until this person shows up in your life.

Affirmations

I will know from within when this assignment has run its course.
I don't need to know the outcome of my relationship. I am safe with my own self.
I am strong enough to love myself first.
I am fed by the light of my inner life.

Prayer to Heal
Addiction to Love

Dear Higher Mind,
Some force within me is chasing
after unrequited love.
Loneliness is closing in on my heart
and I want to find solace in the arms of another.
My heart is stuck on the chord of neediness;
I can't help obsessing about my partner
as I silently implore him to love the self
that I cannot love.

I invite the omnipotence
of your unconditional love
to enter my heart at this moment.
Help me appease the inner child
wailing in pain right now,
surrounding it safely with my own acceptance.
Grant me the stamina to parent my own heart.

May I no longer defer my heart's needs
to another human being. May I be
the determining authority over my worth.
I am willing to be my own lover first so that
I may learn the meaning of true partnership.
Amen.

Visualization

Close your eyes and invite the presence of unconditional love within the walls of your mind and the sacred space of your heart. Now visualize a deep red mist of love wrapped around your heart. Gently place your palms over your heart, allowing the mist to intensify in color to cleanse your heart from self-hatred, unworthiness, and external validation. Feel the freedom that your own love offers you, at any moment. You are undoing the latch to your own love and your source of true power.

Affirmations

I am the heart that I seek.

I embody the love that I desire to experience.

I welcome all of myself, even sadness, self-rejection, and desperation.

I cannot be abandoned. I am always here for myself.

I am the big love I've been waiting for.

Prayer to Transform
The Fear of Commitment

Dear Breath of Divine Grace,
I keep running from my intimate relationships.
I am afraid of losing my heart
and not being able to recover it at will.
If I let my heart loose in my relationship,
it could be shattered at any moment.
I find myself wanting to be my own stern warden.
But I also know that when I try to escape love,
I run away from great joy and growth.

May I realize that only by opening my heart
to myself will I step into emotional safety.
I am the sole power that can add
or take love away from my self.
My darkest fears will turn to light
as I plow through the illusions
blocking the true love that awaits me.

I am always at home in my own heart.
Amen.

VISUALIZATION

Visualize yourself facing you, with a white light coming
from your heart toward the heart of the self you see. Allow
that light to emit a divine cycle of light between your hearts.
As you reconnect with yourself, the fear of losing yourself in
any relationship dissolves. The anxiety of abandonment and
betrayal leave your body as you come to feel how held you are
by your connection to your own heart. You can always return
to the love within you that is love that is love. You are safe
with yourself forever, and the fearful voice that keeps you from
commitment is a shadowy illusion from the past. It is no longer
your reality. Your deep, loving, joyful connection with your
heart is your new reality.

AFFIRMATIONS

I am naturally at home within my heart.
It is safe to feel fear and let it pass through me.
I can let go of control and find peace instead.
My fears are guides for me to return home to myself.
I can never lose my own heart.

Prayer for a
Peaceful Divorce

Dear Soul of Compassion,
From our hearts, we have drawn the conclusion that
divorce is the most loving transition for our family.
It is our highest intention, dear God,
to leave this marital space peacefully and lovingly.
The noble purpose of our relationship remains
although the structure is about to evolve.
Knowing our wounds may be activated
throughout this process, enable our loving intentions
to become our common ground.

Please bless us with clarity so that we may be
guided to walk the highest path as a family.

May we consciously choose to build each other up
rather than tear our egos apart.
May I bring my personal pain into the fold of my own heart
before blaming another.

I trust that love goes with me wherever I go.
I let you take this divorce from here on, dear Creator.
Amen.

Visualization

Bring your spouse into the safe space of your inner vision, holding him or her within a frame of white light before you. Allow yourself to feel the rising tensions as the pain, regrets, and fears of the recent past rise into your physical awareness now. Let those emotions exist in your body. They deserve to be seen and held by you. Honor yourself for choosing to feel the guilt, the blame, and the anger. Now place your hands over your heart and silently repeat to yourself, "I honor us for choosing the brave and true path for our hearts and for the well-being of all involved. I applaud us for our courage in difficult circumstances. I am willing to see that love has to wind around certain experiences to grow in strength and truth. I trust that life is guiding everyone involved in this heartbreak toward a higher pathway. What I forgive in myself will also be forgiven in this relationship. I am coming home to myself, at last, and this renewed relationship with my own soul will be the underlying wisdom and strength of this divorce." The freedom you have just created will invite the exact experiences, teachers, and love that you both need moving forward into the next stage of your lives.

Affirmations

I am a better person for the love I have known in this marriage.
I will let love lead in these grieving times.
I am at peace with this decision.
Forgiveness flows through my heart now.

Meditation II:
Releasing Ego

When I am entangled
in the chaos of ego play,
my mind leads my heart astray,
pushing it to align with judgment
and project lies onto the film of my life.
These egoic thoughts are but a call for love,
so I will let my loving Self recall the
ancient melodies of my soul.
From those sounds comes the light
that restores all love and peace
to my thinking.

PRAYERS FOR
The Self

I place all my quests into
the care of Love.

Prayer for Self-Love

Dear God,
I do not feel love flowing
through my depleted being now.
Although I intellectually understand love,
I do not know how to feel connected with it.

Please help me release the blindfold
of my old beliefs that hide the lovability
of my soul, my body, and my heart.

I am aware that my demeaning thoughts
do not honor the Truth of who I am.
Refresh my inner sight with original purity
so that I may witness myself as you see me.
I need only love
the authentic spirit that I am.

Reveal to me the crystal truth
through which You behold me.
Help me feel the satin cloak of my lovely Self.

I am ready to honor myself in all Your grandeur.
I can feel the murmur of my heart
increasing in love now.
AMEN.

Visualization

See for yourself a river flow of gold honey elixir pouring from the sky onto the crown of your head. Watch as that bright elixir begins to melt over your shoulders, your arms, your chest, your hips, and the rest of your body until you are entirely enveloped in gold. Feel your energy shift as your perception of yourself begins to lift and you feel energized by your new golden presence. That energy is gently dissolving all the doubts, self-loathing, regrets, and your harsh perception of yourself melt into its thick balm of divine love.

Affirmations

My lovability is all I see and feel now.
I embrace all the parts of myself that are hurt.
I am my own wisdom.
God gave me the entire world to bless, so that I may never feel
*   loveless again.*

Prayer for Abundance

Dear Source of All,
I feel constricted by my lack of abundance
as every turn of life seems to draw me
into deeper holes of drought.
My mind is scarred by the scarcity of my past
and it cannot be consoled by my fearful jests.

I love you, sweet river of abundance,
and I trust in your guidance.
Help me return to the wealth that dwelt in me
before my impossible belief in lack arose.

Remind me of my majestic possibilities
as the creator of all that I feel and imagine.
Lift the heavy curtain from my eyes so that I may
be grateful for the abundance flourishing
above me, beneath me, and all around me.

I rejoice in recognizing that my fear of lack
is just my shadow cast from standing
in the way of the Lights of Heaven.
Amen.

Visualization

Visualize yourself sitting outside, on plush, green grass in the middle of a vast field. The grass goes on infinitely and you feel the warmth of the sun as you gently let your palms rest on your lap. Take a few deep breaths to release all tension from your body. On your right, a narrow stream of clear water flows by, its quiet rushing easing all fear and tightness from your being. Now you begin to see currency floating on top of the gentle water; just a few pieces of paper at first, then increasing until you can hardly see the water anymore. As you welcome the abundance flowing towards you, you feel a surge of gratitude in your heart for the abundance now present in your life. The more gratitude you feel, the faster the abundance comes towards you.

Now you lift up your chest toward the bright blue skies and you begin to feel the river of wealth flowing through you. There is a circle of currency flowing in and out, as you give and receive in equal measure with the Source of all well-being. Give yourself a few minutes to dwell in this energy of gratitude, abundance, and joy until you feel totally relaxed and refreshed.

Affirmations

Abundance flows through me to support my good work in the world.
My breath reconnects me to the flow of abundance within me.
The brilliant light within dispels all sense of lack.
I choose to behold a world of joy and infinite giving.

Prayer for Body Image

Dear God,
I feel unattractive
and I cannot love my body as it is.
I desire to be a loving and positive vessel of Truth
and I recognize that I cannot serve
when I despise myself.

Transform my contrite vision of my body
into a sanctified messenger of loving
thoughts and energies.
Help me shed all the strands of judgment
that keep me enrobed in self-hatred and neglect.

I drop all my self-critical thoughts
into your open, loving palms now.
May I use my body and my vitality for purposes
that celebrate the beauty and sacredness
of all living things.

Let my mind's eye maintain
a bright and clear vision of my body
as a transcendent pillar of light that manifests
the wonders of Truth you have instilled in me.
Amen.

VISUALIZATION

Visualize yourself walking on an ancient path of golden stones. You approach a beautiful, ancient temple surrounded by large marble columns, lined with golden sphinxes and torches of fire in between the statues. You walk up the old steps and you enter the temple through a gate overlooked by stone carvings of ancient Goddesses.

Entering the sanctuary, you instantly feel a stream of light coming from the ceiling of the temple. You stand beneath that bright, healing, cleansing light for a few moments, with the palms of your hands facing the light. You let the bright light inform your cells and your energy. You are invited to shed the old vision of yourself and be reborn into the glorious being you have always been. This is your initiation into the highest version of yourself.

Now you keep walking through this large room until you begin to notice steam coming from a large swimming pool underneath a large glass mosaic, reflecting the light emanating from the pool with an iridescent effect. You drop the white robe from your shoulders and enter the gleaming water to cleanse yourself from all your past and current limiting beliefs. As you immerse yourself into the sacred waters, you feel all dark energies drift away from your body, lightening and relaxing you. Gold flecks attach to your hair and skin, as the Goddess within you rises to your physical awareness. She comes through the chambers of your heart and charges your entire body with a powerful current of bright energy, purifying and empowering you with her majestic presence. You see your reflection in an antique, full-body mirror as you go up the steps out of the magical bath. You have been made anew; you are now as radiant as a golden sun.

Affirmations

I don my sacred garment of body confidence now.

I revel in my unique beauty and I am grateful to be myself.

I love and honor the majestic passing of time in my appearance.

I reign as a queen in my inner kingdom, incomparable to anyone.

MEDITATION III:
Mastering Your Thoughts

I can sense the upheaval of unloving thoughts,
and I am aware of the necessity to stop them
before they invade the forefront of my mind.
I turn my awareness over to cosmic wisdom,
the compassionate decision-maker within.
I invoke the intimate presence of my soul
to return my mind to love now.

Prayer for Eating Disorders

Dear Holy Magician,
I come to you now because I despise my body
and all that it represents.
I am told that I am wrong to dislike my shape,
but my body hatred is sharp and acute.
When the vents of my restless pain blow open,
I am dragged down by the need to numb the
emotional aches that bubble within my body.

Help me discern the deeper wound
hidden by my addiction.
May I meet this troubling infection of my soul
with empathy, burning love, and complete honesty.

May I befriend my inner child's unnoticed plea
for love and attention and its cries
digging into my skin
to feed my unclaimed worth.
Remind me that I contain enough love
to honor and soothe this pain with grace.
Amen.

Visualization

Now we are going to dive down into the bleeding wounds of your soul to transform your perception of your body. Visualize yourself in a fetal position, crying on the floor of your bathroom. Allow yourself to feel all the pain that has been waiting to be expressed through your body, asking for acceptance, release, and healing.

An older, brighter, more peaceful version of yourself approaches and touches the inner little girl who feels so much pain and self-loathing, saying: "I am here now. It is over. You are good. You are so lovable, and you can transmute this pain into a greater version of yourself. Your pain is your crown and savior, my child. Let it guide you. You had to be broken open to let more light into you. You are the love you have been looking for and all along, it is your acceptance that you were looking for. Rise now, and feel how beautiful and worthy you are."

And now connect to the feelings that arise in your body. Now you know that you can handle your emotions in the palm of your heart — and that you are never alone on the path of healing and transformation.

Affirmations

I am a soul embodying sacredness.
My soul is a center of love, healing all arising pain.
I am lovable at any size or shape.
I love my body as a sacred vehicle to accomplish good in the world.

Prayer to Release Ingratitude

Dear Source of All,
I see life through a lens of perennial insufficiency.
I hold on tightly to meager resources because
the thought of losing everything terrorizes me.
I think that abundance exists in the Universe
but I don't believe that it works on my behalf.

Help me clear the troubled soot from my consciousness
so that clear generosity may pour into me.

May I appreciate all expressions of wealth
already present in my life so that
my awareness may grow enriched
by sacred gratitude.

Remind me to be thankful for all the gifts in my life,
knowing that gratitude generates plenitude.
Let me feel the healing shower of kindness
fall upon me now.
Amen.

Visualization

See a circle of white light emanating from the center of your stomach, sending out bright and powerful rays of light. It increases in luminosity as you place your hands over that sacred center, feeling a sense of overwhelming peace. You are now connecting to your energetic source of personal abundance and strength. Feel the gratitude as you allow that light to expand outside of you until it encircles the room you are in, sending illumination throughout your home, your street, and your city. You are now at the center of an immense circle of light and your centers of energy are awakened, open, and filled with love.

Affirmations

I behold fullness in everything I see.

Gratitude is the vision through which I see the world.

Generosity meets me everywhere I go.

Prayer for Independence from Approval

Dear Divine Maker,
My self-esteem is collapsing beneath
my crushing need for external validation.
My acts and decisions must always pass through
the needle of worldly acceptance
before I honor them.

Help me to bridge the gap between
my doubtful heart and my trusting soul.
Let my mind breathe in the glow of my soul
to become free from the approval of others.
Lead me home to my heart
to embody my inherent goodness.
May I happily reclaim my divine worth
so that I may see myself in a true light.
I will no longer weaken my personal power
for the sake of approval.
Amen.

VISUALIZATION

Quietly ask yourself:

"Why do I have more trust in the world's opinion of me than
    in my own?"

"Why do I trust others' judgment habitually?"

"Why am I unworthy of trust and respect?"

 "Who told me in the past that I was not purely lovable?"

"Whose voice is coming back when I doubt myself?"

Allow these questions to rest in the silence within you,
then give to them all one answer:

"I let the Love that is my Self shine in me now, showing me
the truth about my personal story, my soul, and all of my life.
I am the ruler over my worth and my power. I no longer defer
my worth to anyone else but to the quiet loving and wise guide
at the center of my heart. And so it is."

AFFIRMATIONS

I go home to my heart to restore my soul.
My trusted source of wisdom is within.
I am my own voice of validation.
No one can change the truth of who I am deeply within.

Prayer to
Let Ourselves Be Seen

Dear Supreme Lover,
I have been reluctant to let myself be seen
for the imperfect person that I am.
The wounds in my heart make me
feel sore, exhausted, and lonely.
My past taught me that the display
of my true emotions would poison love.

I invoke You to pour a river of compassion
down the narrow alleys of my self-perception.

Help me see that vulnerability constitutes my real power.
Help me transcend the need to be perfect now,
and dissolve my hovering shame.
Help me place my truth before the finish line of approval.

I am done fighting the part of me that
strives to be seen and accepted.
My soul is yours to be made whole.
Amen.

Visualization

Choosing to witness the root reasons beneath your feelings of unworthiness, begin a cycle of soft breathing to invite a higher wisdom. Ask yourself: "Why am I afraid to be seen by others? What is the worst thing that could happen if I was fully recognized? What do I not want to show? Whose opinions do I fear the most?"

Breathe white light into your heart to shine truth onto the old stories about your lack of self-worth. Release every anxiety with blessings of love and acceptance. Connect to the original heartbreak scene in your past that began teaching you that you were unworthy of life and of love. As you visualize yourself in that situation, picture an older, brighter version of yourself shining the white healing light onto you, to restore your faith and the life force that left after that painful situation.

Now you are ready to let go of the false stories about yourself that have dictated your unconscious beliefs for far too long. The long-awaited miracle is at the gate of your life now.

Affirmations

My openness is a gift to myself.
Vulnerability is the only way to crack open my hard shell.
It is safe to allow my soul to be seen now.
I am protected by the truth.

Prayer to Feel Complete

Dear Source of Compassion,
I feel incomplete,
with multiple breaches in my self-awareness.
I've allowed experiences from the past
to blemish my view of self.

I'm ready to reclaim my forgotten parts now;
I welcome the vocation of recreating myself
from the rough strokes of my soul.

I am the sovereign of my persona:
I consciously decide what enters and departs my mind.
I shine love upon the shadows of my psyche
so that they may become healing suns.
I am willing to rebirth myself into a whole person
who finds herself worthy of unconditional love.
Amen

VISUALIZATION

Picture a light blue mist of unconditional love flowing towards your heart. As it swirls into you, exhale energies of tension, doubt, and lack. Repeat to yourelf, "I inhale unconditional love and I exhale tension and self-doubt." Repeat that cycle of breaths for a few moments.

By now, you can begin to see a bright white light glowing from within, extending from your heart space and enveloping you. Now feel yourself expanding into that space of grace, experiencing a confidence and a love greater than what you've ever known. All the shadows within yourself are eliminated by this incandescent light. You bask in the most complete shining presence you have ever known.

You are free; You are light; You are love.

AFFIRMATIONS

I am complete in my own right.
I live deeply seated in my inner world.
I am grateful for the lifeline to my soul.
I fulfill myself with honor and integrity.

Prayer for Self-Worth

My Beloved Father,
I recognize that I feel little esteem
for the self of my past, the self that was denied love.
I have placed more faith in the world's perception
of myself than in your holy creation.

Today, I see the past no more.
I commit to seeing myself as the holy extension
of Life itself, and I will not let the world defile
my heart any longer.

I will honor what You created
while infusing love into the shades of my conscience.
Help me reconnect with my worth as your child.
Stir the brilliance of my gifts so that
I may better serve the world.

I come empty-handed unto You,
willing to embody a bold new vision of myself.
Amen.

VISUALIZATION

See a golden thread of light streaming from the deep sky to the top of your head. That flow of light taps into the Source of all energy. The light descends into your heart, cleansing all sensations of worthlessness and littleness.

Now allow yourself to remember a time in your childhood when you felt unworthy of love. Perhaps it was a parent, a family member, a close friend who made you believe that you were unworthy of love. The first situation that comes to mind will do. See yourself as that child and connect with the emotions that you felt at the time. Call upon that light to swirl around you and the person who projected their own uncertainties and fears upon you. Their rejection of you had nothing to do with you. It had everything to do with their own unhealed traumas. Allow that light to soothe you in the places that were hurt and betrayed. The light will heal you and bring you back to wholesomeness. In this light, you forgive the individual for projecting wrongly onto you and you forgive yourself for believing their illusion for that long.

AFFIRMATIONS

I am love incarnate.
My impeccable worth precedes my deeds.
I have nothing to prove to the world.
I am entitled to miracles as an expression of the Divine.

Prayer to
Take Our Power Back

Dear I Am That I Am,
I feel powerless over my world.
My life force is running back and forth
between my past and future,
and I cannot hold my center.
My power to choose again is confined in my ego's prison,
and I feel that I have no leverage on my reality.

Yet, I know that the enlightened part of my mind
lives within the sacred power of surrender.

Please help me accept that I do not control
what comes to me, but I do choose
how I experience everything.
I ask you for a fresh pair of eyes today
so that I may assign the most loving meaning
to all that arises.

I am willing to recognize
that that my greatest power lies in embracing
the perfect order beneath all outcomes.
I cease attempting to control life
to let my power be returned to me.
Amen.

Visualization

Closing your eyes with hands upon your heart, connect with the feeling of being a powerless victim of life. Allow all that sadness and helplessness to be felt in your heart and in your body. With a few deep breaths, welcome a rush of light into the contracted space of these feelings. Keep breathing brilliance into that limited space until you feel an expansion, a widening of possibilities, a surge of power within you straightening your spine. The breath of renewal is transforming the sorrow of powerlessness into trust, peace, and joy, now. You now recognize that YOU are in charge of your interior world and its reigning energies. Feel gratitude for the opportunity to transform your perception as a victim into an empowered being in the service of love.

Affirmations

I am in charge of my energetic state.
I am the guardian of my heart.
My bliss is a few breaths away from fear.
The power of creation is always moving through me.

Prayer to Alleviate Depression

Dear God,
I am at my wit's end,
and I have not even the slightest hope
in my sick and twisted existence.
I fear that my future is going to be just like the past
and I am reliving my deepest pains every single day.
I feel alone and abandoned by all life;
I can't overcome my dragging sadness.

Empower me to doubt my hopeless heart.
In this precious moment,
I am willing to consider being wrong
about the absence of possibilities.

For the time being, I'm willing to let a
dangling star of joy point me toward the future.
If my imagination can dream a different world,
then it can draw forth a healed reality.
Amen.

VISUALIZATION

Visualize a navy blue door in front of you. It is the door to your imagination, and now you turn the handle to open it. There are vasts fields of bright sunny flowers, potent green grass, and sparkles of joy floating in the air. Nothing is impossible or limited here. The Sun is shining brighter than ever before and you enjoy its warmth on your face.

Now invite a vision of yourself in the middle of a bright green pasture, one year from today. If anything were possible, what would it look like in your life? What would you be doing? What would your love and friendships look like? Your face is beaming with happiness and contentment as you stand in the open field with wide open arms, blessed by life all around you. You make the commitment to trust in that vision and you dwell in the feelings it engenders for a few more moments. You see hope now. You have just experienced a brighter version of your life, and what it can become.

AFFIRMATIONS

I replace my weariness with willingness.
I honor my sadness for its messages as I move forward with hope.
I focus on the range of things that can change.
Every feeling is always evolving to a more powerful, healing energy.

Prayer to Embrace Aging

Dear Mother Goddess,
As I walk along the timeline of my life
I find myself resisting growing old.
I look at my face and the lazy skin irks me.
My bones are grinding, crumbling.
My body is ignoring my commands.

Yet, I want to find the grace that grows with time.

May my radiance come from gratitude
for every day that is given to me.
May my inner state of quietude glow from within;
I am willing to make confidence and serenity
the new sexy.
May my allure rest in the
elegance of my earned wisdom.
My beauty begins where my light shines.
Amen.

Visualization

Begin to see for yourself a swirl of silver, shimmering glitter
rising from the ground to enrobe your feet. Breathing deeply,
feel that vortex of glitter move up along your calves, your
knees, and your thighs. The bright wrap now travels upward to
cover your hips, waist, chest, and arms. Allow this shimmering
whirlwind to envelop your neck and face until your entire body
glistens with light. Now you get to celebrate a holier vision
of your physical body. It is a vessel to bring forth goodness,
wisdom, and grace that only comes with maturity. You can go
about your day now with the bright consciousness of
true beauty.

Affirmations

The passing of time through my body magnifies my inner radiance.
My beauty resides in the love expressed by my soul.
Serenity and wisdom give me a timeless elegance.

MEDITATION IV:
Releasing Expectations

When I cling to specific outcomes,
my center of light is scattered and
I perceive nothing but my own projections.
Help me release the expectations
I have built from mad hopes
and self-serving dependency.
I surrender my most cherished outcomes
in favor of the highest unfoldment for my life.
I clear the way for unknown possibilities
to be shown to me in sacred timing.

PRAYERS FOR
Family

*The family is a pre-arranged
constellation of spiritual growth.*

Prayer for Motherhood

Dear God,
I come humbly before you
as the mother of my beloved children
and witness for all the children of this world.

Thank you for weaving your living light
into the sanctuary of my womb
so that I could host the gift of life.
I do not know how to be a perfect mother
and I am often ridden with guilt.

May I not project onto my children
the bruises of my own childhood
but instead let your unconditional love
flow through me and fill their hearts.
Draw upon the blank page of my mind
the ways in which I can mirror their magnitude,
helping them use the strength that is not their own
but dwells within them always.
May they strive not for acceptance
from the world, but thrive in the
inner fire of their own genius.

May my life be their most potent reminder
that love is who they are and that it
will always sustain them.
Amen.

Visualization

Close your eyes, take a few deeps breaths in through the nose and out the mouth. Continue that gentle cycle of breaths until all tensions dissipate from your upper body.

Allow yourself to witness all the negative thoughts you have held since you first became a mother. Kindly welcome these condemnations, and see how you have unfairly expected perfection from yourself.

Now pour all these unloving thoughts into a golden chalice standing on a white altar before you. As they depart from your mind and heart, a radiant elixir of pink light appears all around. Breathe in that loving pink energy and let it flow into your heart, replacing the judgments you have plastered on your identity as a mother. Breathe in that light and breathe it out... allowing it to cascade down into the chalice that contains all the guilt and self-loathing that you have dropped in there.

Under the light of forgiveness, give yourself and your children the gift of release. You are now empowered to continue the journey of motherhood with divine inspiration, blessing your children with your own confidence and strength.

Affirmations

Through my inner fulfillment, my children witness the power of joy.
The gift of unconditional love is the greatest gift I can give my children.
I trust my motherly instinct to guide my children.
My maternal love is greater than all the material gifts of the world.

Prayer for Daughters
Without Fathers

Dear Sacred Father,
There is a fatherless melancholy lodged in my heart.
I am desperate to find the masculine love
that was robbed from me as a little girl.
I have been swimming in an ocean of loneliness,
trying to cling to any male attention that I can reach.
My inner little girl aches to be seen, and
drags me towards deceptive forms of interim love.

I am not in control of my own love impulses.

Free me from this hunger; comfort my head
that was never held against a father's chest.
Bless my restless mind so that it thrives
in the stronghold of my own soul,
where I am accepted for once and for all.
The gift of building my own identity in the present
isa gracious honor I receive from my past.

I give up my orphan story now.
Amen.

VISUALIZATION

Together, we are going to soothe and comfort the little girl in you who never felt loved by her father. Begin to visualize the hurt and lonely child you once were, looking down and ready to weep away all her aching pain. Your shoulders are hunched and your eyes are gloomy, on the verge of heavy tears. Now kneel down in front of your younger self, lift this sad child's chin and speak these words, with a loving light from Heaven shining from your eyes into her eyes:

"Your father is no longer in your life and it is a painful separation. You didn't do anything wrong and he did not leave you because you are unworthy. His absence has nothing to do with you. You are a beloved child, worthy of the most glorious love in life. You are a magical being. The void you feel inside can be filled by the love that I am showing to you now. Your heart is calling for you to come home with me. You are always at my center. I couldn't live without you, and you are not alone or abandoned. You are the key to me, and you are so loved."

Take a deep breath and exhale, releasing all the blocks and shame that held your childhood pain in place. You are free. Welcome back to you.

AFFIRMATIONS

I am worthy of the strongest form of love.
I heal my old worthlessness by accepting, then releasing it.
I feel love and respect growing within me, free of dependence.
I live my new definition moment-by-moment.

Prayer for Fatherhood

Dear Father on High,
I ask for a blessing upon my calling
as a father of your embodied souls.
Grant me the archetypal gifts of a
man's power so that I may bring Heaven
into the material world for my family.

May the resonance of my heart
lead me to be a noble protector,
a righteous provider,
and an example of gallantry.

Strengthen my resolve to be present for my children
And impart to them the gift of balanced masculinity.
Drown my fears with the flow of courage,
devotion, and persistence every day.

May I show compassion toward my own emotions
as a show of masculine strength.
May my heart and mind as a father
be driven by divine will so that
my life may shine with almighty Light.
Strengthen within me the flames of
integrity and faith.
Amen.

VISUALIZATION
for Father/Child Bonding

Sit in a comfortable position and close your eyes. Take a few breaths in and out of your mouth and continue that breathing cycle for two minutes.

Now invite within your mind an image of you holding your child in your arms as a baby. Your infant is staring at you as it rests on your forearms. As he or she looks straight into your eyes, you smile. You are looking into each other's soul for a few minutes, as the recognition comes back into your awareness. You have known and loved that child for a very long time, and the remembrance is now entering your heart. A warm mantel of comfort enwraps the both of you as your baby smiles back at you.

Even if you never really felt close to your child as an infant, you can still go back to that time and refresh the bond that was never quite whole.

AFFIRMATIONS
I can achieve my dreams as a man and be an example
    for my children.
I have everything I need to conquer my past.
I am confident in my ability to love my child.
I am superior to my doubts and my heart is valiant.
Every day, I become a more reliable and loving father.

Prayer to Heal
the Fear of Abandonment

Dear Higher Power,
My heart is defiled and there is no hope
of holding it together anymore.
I am abandoned once again and
I cannot seem to prevent this malignant cycle.

Every heart I love bails out.
I can't do this anymore. I can no longer
expose my heart to the raw elements of life.

May I see that feeling abandoned
is a buried plea for love from my inner child.
Whenever I hand her off to others to love,
I forsake responsibility as my own loving caretaker.
May I no longer disown my emotions
but instead infuse them with tender compassion.

I am willing to assume my role as my own loving parent
to tend to the places in me that were never embraced.
Sweet inner child,
Welcome home to your true heart,
my very own.
Amen.

VISUALIZATION

Closing your eyes to enter your interior field of grace, gently invite a vision of yourself as a child. Trusting the first image that appears, see your adult self kneeling down in front of this innocent child and placing your hands upon its shoulders, sending love and reassurance into its frightened, insecure eyes. Now witness a healing balm of pink, unconditional love emanating from your very own heart, moving toward the child until he or she is wrapped in the pink, loving mist.

Now utter these words to the beautiful light being before you: "Dear inner child, I am here for you. I will no longer abandon you. I will no longer defer your care, well-being, and emotional safety to any other. I will honor your sacred essence and I will always honor your voice. You no longer need to fear, dear child. I love you, just as you are."

AFFIRMATIONS

When I feel hurt, I can soothe and heal it in my own loving hands.
I can connect with my own heart to find the love I think I need
  from others.
I invite unconditional love to hold me in my pain of abandonment.
I am the love that takes care of itself.

PRAYER FOR THE
WOUNDED INNER CHILD

Dear Tender Father,
My heart is chasing after thrill rides of happiness
but I never reach the shores of true fulfillment.
I've been trying to escape a faraway voice inside me,
wailing in despair.

That little girl doesn't know who to turn to.
She has to control everyone around her to feel safe.
She is tired from usurping love
from anyone and everyone.

I am ready to let her heart be healed,
at last.

Help me attend to the imprints of lovelessness
that branded her childhood.
May I reach through time and space
to console my inner child
with all the blessings and reassurance
that I deserved.

May she always feel safe with me.
May I witness all her pains with patience
so that she can come forward safely
into the light of love.
AMEN.

Visualization

Bring into the forefront of your mind the image of yourself as a child. He or she is nervous and has to be invited more than once. In the child's eyes you see pain, crushed hopes, the fear of exposure and betrayal. Now place your hands upon your heart and say to yourself: "I am so sorry for everything you have been through. I am never going to leave you. You are safe and loved with me. You are seen for who you are; you can express all your fears and feelings and still be loved. The weight and wait of loneliness is over. I will never abandon you. I am yours forever. You can rest in my heart and in my arms, dear child. I love you unconditionally."

Bathed in a bright white light, you hold your heart for a few moments. It feels warm, at peace, and at home with you.

Affirmations

I am the holy space in which all hurts are healed.
When I bless my inner child, my soul grows in power.
I am the source of safety and love for my core child.

Prayer to Heal
Emotional Abuse

Dear Physician of the Soul,
My heart feels bruised.
Unhealed individuals projected their
excruciating wounds onto my mind and body.
Every day, I would be the subject
of their hatred towards me
and my heart crumbled from the pain.
I allowed humiliation to define my identity
and I've not known how to break that spell.

Please help me refuse these piercing projections.
Wash away all aggressions with your healing breath.

Help me draw forth my true self,
too long stifled by abuse,
recovering the intelligence and beauty I own.

I invoke a holy revolution to enter my inner world
so that your love may erase the lies forced into me.
May I be free forever from the dark figures
that once danced around
the periphery of my true Self.
AMEN.

Visualization

Invite your bright, brilliant soul to appear as a delightful circle of love and pure light around you. Now allow the most cruel thoughts about yourself to rise into awareness. It is safe to let them come up because you are not alone in this process. As you review these thoughts, begin to feel a warmth in the mid-section of your body. You see a bright yellow light rising up to your heart center. This healing light lifts and carries all your painful thoughts through the heart, letting them leave you through the exhalations of steady breaths. Now release these thoughts to be integrated into the eternal truth of your soul, where they will be transformed into pure love. When you breathe in, that love returns to you. Repeat this cycle until all your unloving thoughts no longer have a charge in you.

Affirmations

My eternal soul is my true identity.
I can soothe my own heart with love.
I have the inalienable right to be loved.
I am constantly evolving from my pain.

MEDITATION V:
Returning to the Present Moment

Mental chatter encumbers
my clarity of heart and vision.
I call on the presence
of heaven within
to awaken me now.
As I place my attention on
the circulation of my breath,
all awareness of past and future
collapses into present time.
I feel the pulse of my heart
quietly echoing the
murmurs of my soul.
I feel peace soaking through my flesh
as I ground my mind and heart
in the now.

PRAYERS FOR
The World

*The most important spiritual practice
is the appreciation of life as it is now.*

Prayer for Happiness
In the Workplace

Dear God,
I loathe my workplace; I am filled with dread
as I wake up to begin my workday.
The reigning ambience is toxic and
I feel my soul drowning in it.
My resistance affects my energy
and my ability to be effective in my profession.
I do not know how to get past this.

May I accept the guidance
of my own wiser self
within the confines of this occupation.
I pledge to dissolve all judgments
about my source of income,
my co-workers, and my superiors.
Bless them all with inspiration.
May I be a vessel through which you uplift
the people I encounter every day.
I recognize that my true purpose
is to mirror Heaven on Earth
while not expecting perfection
of anyone, including myself.
I will remember that anywhere I work
is a realm of opportunities
to bring forth more love.
Amen.

Visualization

In the very center of your heart, picture your workplace: the parking lot, your office or desk, and the office of your boss. There is a cloud of bright, rosy light hovering over the building. The pink light is joined by a white light, enveloping the workplace until every corner, hallway, and office is basking in a healing glow. As you enter, breathe in the pink and white light through your nose, letting it travel into the center of your heart and down into your solar plexus. All blocks of resistance, fear of losing your employment, and other toxic thoughts are now dissolved by that divine blend of healing light. Connect with gratitude for the positive gifts that your work offers you, knowing you will be guided out of your current situation in perfect timing for all involved.

Affirmations

I am a force for good everywhere I go.
My work is an inspired ministry to work miracles.
I am told everything I need to know when I silence my ego and
*   open my heart.*
The blessings that I bring to work are far greater than the challenges
*   of my profession.*

Prayer to Carry Forth Our Dreams

Dear Life,
Preciously held in the middle of my mind,
I imagine my most cherished dream.
As I behold the depth and breadth of it,
I feel powerless before its grandeur.

Attaining my dream seems insurmountable.
My heart is jammed with fears of failure.

Unwind my mind, dear Life, so that
I do not reject myself before the Muse
completes her designs through me.

By affirming the love She vests in me,
I heal my internal circuits of fear
to let life weave miracles on my behalf.

May your grace dissolve my doubts
so that I can welcome a creative tide of
trust within my heart.
Amen.

Visualization

Invite images of your most cherished dream to arise in your mind. No pictures or ideas are forbidden. Allow your imagination to run large, wild, and limitless. Give yourself the permission to dream freely in this space of love and silence. Witness all the feelings that are evoked by these images. Begin a cycle of deep inhales and exhales to quiet your mind so that your most creative and inspired mind may join you. What images do you see? How are you feeling? What are you saying? Where are you?

Name every emotion that arises — Joy, Fulfillment, Devotion, or whatever arises for you. Name the work that you are doing, and see those names brighten and shimmer within. This very vision will guide you past the inner slums of fear and doubt, and you will grow into your dream every single day. Now place your hands over your heart, sealing the dream with love and trusting that it will be taken care of, for the highest good of this world.

Affirmations

My dreams are the blueprint of my purpose here.
My soul speaks to me through imagination.
The Universe actualizes itself through me.
I was born with the abilities necessary to realize my potential.

PRAYER TO FIND OUR PURPOSE

Dear God,
I come unto you empty-handed,
with a lost heart.
I feel useless and my life seems
without an honorable purpose.

I wish to be used by your higher mind
for the betterment of the world.
I bow my head in humble surrender,
as I ask you to turn my awareness
towards the special function you
would have me fulfill.

I will strive to make myself spacious within
so that I may lovingly host your destiny for me.
I am willing to be a spokesperson of your Truth.

May the manifestation of my sacred pledge
to bring forth love into the world
reflect your Will, always.
AMEN.

Visualization

See yourself seated before a small round table in the middle of a white room. On this golden table, you notice a scroll of parchment rolled up and tied with a white ribbon. This scroll holds the information that you need to fulfill your special function on this Earth. On this day, you will be given what you need to know to begin moving the wheels of your holy destiny. With a loving hand, untie and slowly unroll the ancient beige parchment, revealing your name at the top right corner. As you read the rest of the page, you begin to feel the brilliance and generosity of the unique gifts that you have been given; you feel ecstatic joy and disbelief in your heart. This destiny was written just for you and you are now overwhelmed with gratitude for life. You will keep these words in your heart and carry them with you everywhere. Write down the words, images, and sensations that arise. Trust what comes up so that it may deliver the fullness of its plan for you.

Affirmations

I give my life to God to use.
I attract opportunities to work miracles all the time.
The moment I begin sharing my truth, those who need my work begin to look for me.
I trust that my truth will elevate the world.

Prayer for Peace
In the World

Dear God,
The world shakes with violence,
sadness, and incomprehension.
Some shattered hearts are
blind to your omnipresent love.

Please help me remember that I cannot
fix the world, but I can deepen my own
awareness of love so that my soul becomes
a mirror of peace for my brothers and sisters.
Please hold my mind in the perennial peace
of your Kingdom, so that I may witness
the melodrama of this mortal world with a
radical and loving consciousness.

Lead us out of the descending spiral
of defense and attack so that we may share
the splendor of each other's innocence.
May peace and renewed hope prevail over
the recurrence of our weary sadness.
Amen.

Visualization

Aware of the habitual darkness hovering over the world,
we breathe deeply from our center until we see sparks of light
breaking through the clouds of doubt and despair. The light
intensifies until the earth is enveloped by a miraculous, dense
coat of bright, healing peace. We begin to feel the weightless
presence of that peace first upon our shoulders, dropping down
through us until all tension and fear depart from our bodies,
leaving behind only a profound, imposing stillness. Feeling
weightless and infinitely spacious within, we have become
the profound peace that the world needs.

Affirmations

I am the presence of peace itself.
My radical love stands radiant in the midst of fear.
Peace extends from me as a new kind of power.
I am appointed as a messenger of peace.

Meditation VI:
Achieving Spiritual Clarity

I am committed to feeling a bond
with each person I meet,
respecting my own integrity,
and enacting the transforming
energies of love and compassion.
I devote myself to making wise,
blessed choices based on perceiving
without judgment.
I release the need to know why
things happen as they do,
and surrender my expectations
of how my days should go
or how others should behave.
I choose to turn my doubts
into spiritual opportunities,
knowing that I am perfectly guided
toward what I need.
As I journey ito my inner reality,
I realize that I am
perfectly supported for today.
My dreams are being carried
in this very moment
by the mysteries of love.

PRAYERS FOR
The Inner Life

*Prayer connects your heart
to the heart of the Sacred.*

Prayer to Connect with the Divine Feminine

Dear Ancient Mother,
I have sealed the gates of my heart
to protect myself and disconnect
from my vulnerability.
I am afraid to appear weak
if I let myself be fully seen.

I desire to regain the
unconditional compassion,
cosmic softness, and sensual radiance
of my sacred femininity.
Teach me to reign gently
over the treasures of my heart, so that
its sacred chambers may birth
a myriad of miracles.

Invoke the Goddess within me
so that I may birth the
flood of Her compassion into the world.
Breathe into my chest
the powers of Heaven and Earth
so that I may become the valiant and
noble woman I was born to be.
Amen.

Visualization

Place your hands over your womb. Feel a warm sensation as you see a red glow in the center of your womb growing brighter, and ascending toward the sacred space of your heart. As the red river makes its transcendent journey upward, it opens the internal circuits of your self and it heals all your limiting beliefs, hard knots of self-condemnation, and open wounds of fear. The crimson energy swirls through every chamber of your heart, activating the brilliance of the Divine Feminine to charge every cell within you with purifying love and nurturance. You allow that red firmament of feminine life force to dwell within you for a few moments until you feel a surge of strength, confidence, and peace.

Affirmations

I am the queen of my own heart.
I rule myself with compassion and courage.
I am confident in my soft energy.
I allow myself to be a womb of vulnerable compassion.

Prayer for Surrender

Dear God,
My soul stands nakedly vulnerable
at the crossroads of my blurry destiny
and the scalding fears in my head.
My life is being dismantled and my hopes
are dangling outside my heart right now.
I can feel the purging light of your love healing
the bruised patches of my fearful self,
but I cannot see a clear path ahead.
I used to think that you owed me happiness.
I used to think that you would grant me my wishes.
I have treated you like a genie
who would comply with my caprices.

Please help me renounce all the wishes
that do not serve my highest good
so that miracles may arrive with your perfect timing.
I do not know where to set foot tomorrow,
but I yearn to set my heart on your will
and nothing else.

You owe me nothing, dear God,
because your plan for my happiness
is already in place.
Amen.

Visualization

See a shimmering white altar in the center of your mind. Bring all the desires and preferred outcomes that you have been holding within to the bright light glowing at the very center of the altar. The light grows upward, like a vortex, until it engulfs the entire room, and your desires dissolve into the light. Now that same vortex is shining in your mind, a beautiful empty vessel ready to receive all that the Divine has already elected for your self-realization. Now you step forward onto the path laid out before, leading toward true bliss and the best version of your future.

Affirmations

Everything coming to me is an experience sent by the Divine to reveal pure happiness.

I trust in the Divine unfolding of all situations in the present moment.

I drop into the open emptiness of my mind so that spirit may lead me.

Every event is cultivated to lead me back to my happiness within.

Prayer for Forgiveness

Dear Mystical Womb,
I come unto your heart to help me
release the grievances that cloak my heart.
I have finally arrived at the dire edge
of my guilt and anger.

My resentment is tied to this individual
(_____)
to whom I feel attached
by cords of pain and love.

I recognize that my heart will not be free
until the love is purified.
I welcome into my mind the image of this person,
who is my forgiveness teacher in this moment.
The bright image grows in luminescence at my center.

The incandescence of love shines away
the brittle shadows of the past.
Dear _____,
I bless you with the light of forgiveness
to experience happiness, inner strength,
and a chorus of miracles acclaiming
our liberation together.
Amen.

Visualization

Bring into the center of your awareness the image of the person you resent. You walk up to each other and begin holding hands. You both utter words of surrender and regret for the pain of the past. As you gaze at each other, a bright ball of light descends upon the both of you, pulling you together in a sphere of healing and transformative light. You behold the holy light entering your bodies until there isn't a cell left that is not brilliant and transparent. No bitter thoughts remain untamed by love. You become one in love and all past shadows are released. You feel the wounds that led them to wound you and all anger dissipates from your heart, from your throat, and from your mind. You now feel only love and compassion towards that person. Rejoice in your freedom and the increase in love that now blesses the both of you.

Affirmations

I extend forgiveness to myself for all I have chosen to think.
I bless and drop my loveless judgments now.
My heart beats in the flow of forgiveness.
My cells vibrate with the joy of release.

Prayer for
Strength and Courage

Dear God,
I hear the echoes of my painful past
and the mean mockeries of my old self
challenging my strength.
In vain, I attempt to ignore the critic in me,
but it seems that my faith is
rolling down the hills of my heart.
Infuse your elixir of courage
into the whirlpool of my soul,
so that I may feel your will
manifest through me.

Help me feel your steely strength in my very bones,
and the power of your love kissing my every cell.
Bless my mind with clarity so that my thoughts
may be catapulted past the broken spectres of fear.
What exists truly and eternally is sourced from you only,
dearest Life, and so is my power to bear witness
to all that is loving and true.

In you I abide forever with the
light of all worlds.
Amen.

Visualization

See yourself sitting cross-legged on the side of a dormant volcano. A swirl of red energy arising beneath you creates a perfect glow of warm, intense energy all around. You feel the indomitable strength of the Earth rise through you, straightening your spine, energizing your entire body. Allow the electricity of courage to flow up through you as you raise your eyes to the heavens, thanking the Universe for the armor of courage and strength holding you up now.

Affirmations

*I accept myself for having created ripples of fear,
    knowing I can always change my perceptions.*
*I am not afraid because I was birthed to bring forth my
    authentic truth.*
I have an unlimited flow of courage in the center of my soul.
I practice sacred strength a little bit more every day.

Prayer to Let Go of Fear

Dear God,
I feel a rocky mass of fear
sitting atop my stomach, and I cannot see
beyond the worst-case scenarios I've invented.
Once upon a time, I chose the role of the victim
who was powerless over her own thoughts.
I dispel that aura from me for once and for all.

Please help me reverse my thinking
and remember my ancient power of faith.
Please immerse my mind in your loving presence
until it becomes one with Light, one with Love.

Restore my heart to the frank awareness
of limitless compassion, sweeping
all fearful distortions from every corner
of my mind.

My fears are washed away from my body
and I am free to walk towards the future
that awaits me.
Amen.

VISUALIZATION

See yourself sitting on a hot, golden dune of sand with a faint
mist of gray surrounding you. This is the aura of your fears.
Call forth a bright light from the deepest part of your heart,
which is also at the center of the universe. As the light expands
from within, the gray cloud of fear rapidly dissolves. Your heart
rises fearlessly, opening itself towards the blue sky. Your fears
vanish and only the Truth of Love remains in you. You can now
witness the fearful thoughts arising in your mind but you no
longer hold onto them.

AFFIRMATIONS

The story of my fears ends now.
The bright rays of my heart dissolve the gloom of my anxiety.
I call upon the unlimited power of Divinity to choose loving thoughts.
When I choose a loving thought, I create beauty and miracles.

Prayer to Increase
Creative Inspiration

Dear Creator of All That Is,
My soul yearns to birth a work of love
but I feel depleted of creative inspiration.

I turn to my interior musings to find nothing
but bitter criticism of myself.

Please open the gateways of my heart
to a forgiving, creative flow.
May the sparks of your genius
descend into my mind to shape
divine imagination into form.

From now on,
I make myself available to receive
all the mysteries of consciousness that inspire
grace, beauty, and healing.

May the Muse decorate my mind with
resplendent jewels of deep magic.
Bless my process so that my heart may
release all outcomes of my artistic work.
Amen.

VISUALIZATION

In the center of your mind, see a dazzling white canvas covering a large wall, surrounded by a halo of sparkling lights. Begin a cycle of deep breaths in and out the nose as you ask, "Dear Muse, what would you have me bring into form? How would have me use my energy to birth a work of art? How can I nurture my creativity today?"

Allow yourself to be patient through this process as the Muse will drop its ideas, inspirations, images when it deems appropriate and divinely timed. Behold the shapes, colors, and words that begin to appear on that white canvas. Open your eyes and take notes.

AFFIRMATIONS

I am a creative force in motion.

When I let go of the outcome of my work, magic enters my mind and creates with me.

When I let go of perfectionism, what I am meant to create comes easily.

My imagination is the gateway of divine inspiration.

MEDITATION VII:
Invoking the Goddess

I come humbly at your sacred feet
to activate our connection.
I invoke your queenly presence into my heart.
Please pour your mysteries into
the chambers of my willing heart.
I wish to be a presence of unconditional love,
sending out the calls of the Holy Mother everywhere.
Please enter my mind, my body, and my heart
to anoint them with the mists of your
mystical feminine energies.
From this day on, I will hold myself
as a sacred daughter of the Goddess
and as a mystical mother of all life.
Infuse my womb with your currents
of Feminine voltage.
Fill my mind with the holy wisdom
you received from the ancient ones,
dear Holy She.

Prayer to Meet Our Soul

Dear God,
I yearn to meet the pure energy that is my soul.
I can intellectually visualize its essence
but I do not know how to let it take root in me.
I want to tap into that unceasing light so that
I may love far beyond the limitations
of my thinking mind.

Walk me onto the throne of my soul.

Guide me to fuse with its amplitude,
its quarks and quirks,
its certitudes and beatitudes.

May I feel my soul's blasts of
unconditional love for me
and all of life's creatures.
May I finally be free
from all the needs enchaining me
to trivial approval and illusory comfort in life.
My soul is a pearl of infinite wisdom.
Amen.

Visualization

Within your mind, see a large solar disk detaching itself from your heart center. Still attached to the heart through a narrow tunnel of light, watch the brilliant disk grow larger and larger until it becomes as large as the Sun itself. In that light, you can let go of everything you've thought you needed to be worthy of love, attention, or approval. You liberate yourself from shame, and let yourself be seen as who you truly are, with all your majestic wounds, wild dreams, and beaming aspirations. In the light of your soul, you feel warmly at home, with original joy bubbling within at the simple idea of being alive and open to the great plan that life has scripted for you.

Affirmations

I merge with my bright soul as I drop all dark self-judgments.
It is safe to be seen for what I am.
My soul is the source of infinite wisdom and unconditional love.
My soul is the holiest spot on Earth.

Prayer to Invite Inner Peace

Dear Divine Mother,
My mind paces restlessly through the corridors
of my troubled past and anxious future.
I cannot feel peace.

My mind feels pulled in aimless directions.
My diaphragm contracts against my breath
in anxiety.

Slip into my mind,
and walk me back to a state of peace.
Sweep your grace over my guilt
and wipe clean all projections that
deny the potential of this present moment.

May I focus on the gift of being alive,
and behold all the ways
in which I am perfectly provided for.
Amen.

Visualization

See yourself in the midst of a field of multicolored roses, petunias, and lilies; there are flowers all around you. The sun is shining its warmth upon your face as you gently close your eyes to dive into the fields of grace in your inner world. Now picture a white dove flying from above and perching itself upon your shoulder. She smells of the lily of the valley and her claws are gently placed on your right shoulder. You respond, "I thank you, dear life, for sending me your messenger of peace so that I may invite peace within me."

The sweet dove is holding a rolled up square piece of paper in its beak, which it drops onto your lap. You gently grab it and begin to write down a list of all the things that are inspiring fear and anxiety in you. All of them. Place the folded paper onto your lap and the dove will take off, grabbing the list with its claws and flying toward the Sun. The anxiety is gone and only bright joy remains bubbling inside your heart and soul.

Affirmations

Peace is the tone of my mind.
I let peace define my thoughts.
My soul is the bearer of all good news.
My inner stillness rules my awareness.

PRAYER FOR UNCONDITIONAL LOVE

Dear Field of Grace,
I have placed limits upon love because
I do not yet know the perfected state of my soul.
Raise my awareness to a level of consciousness
where nothing remains but the pure, gleaming
light of everything that I am.

I invoke your acceptance to smother every fold
of fear, shame, and judgment within me.

As I fall into the abyss of my soul,
may I also fall deeply in love with myself.

I will no longer sink in realms of thought
that forsake the inner marriage of my heart and soul.
I let the cloud of my mind become
a resting chamber of rose petals,
where only love flourishes.
AMEN.

Visualization

See and breathe in a stream of light blue light, watching it enter your nostrils and travel upward. Its purpose is to catch all the debris of self-doubt, fear, and shame that litters your mind. As it descends into your chest, clearing your heart space, the light changes to red whenever it removes a particle of unloving energy. Allow this vapor of unconditional love to absorb the last clusters of emotional resistance anywhere within you. The flow of purifying light rises and departs as you exhale what you no longer need, opening yourself to the experience of unconditional love.

Affirmations

I raise my vibration by accepting myself unconditionally.
I transcend my shadows when I witness them
    with non-judgmental love.
There is nothing in me unworthy of understanding.
When I seek to understand myself, love for all follows.

Prayer for Daily Gratitude

Dear Holy Grace,
My heart is full of gratitude this evening.
I am thankful for all that transpired today,
including the hard lessons and hurdles
that forged my strength in a deeper way.

I offer you my disappointments,
my judgments, my doubts,
and my missteps from the day
so that they shine a light upon
what I need to love within myself.

Let me feel the sacred guidance that will
keep me on the steady path of my destiny.

Infuse your sweet wisdom into my perception
so that I may awaken with a new vision tomorrow,
and bless me to have a peaceful rest.
AMEN.

Visualization

In the quiet space of meditation, ask yourself, "What were my charged emotions today? What events triggered anger, sadness, hopelessness, or shame for me?" Sit with these emotions without trying to change them or make them go away. Accept everything that you have felt, and introduce these companions of the day to your timeless friends of Compassion, Love, and Forgiveness. They will accept everyone they meet, reminding you that no feelings are wrong and there are no "right" feelings that must be experienced in order to be loved. Everything being created in your life is there for the best possible reasons. You are entrusted into the care of the Sacred Universe. Now let a warm blanket of gratitude cover you, enveloping your heart, smiling as you bow to the completion of this day. You were given another day to live, and for that, you are grateful.

Affirmations

I close this day with peace, gratitude, and joy.
I am at peace with today's gifts from life.
I am not what I did today; I am the love that I extended.
All events are designed to return me to my inner light.

Prayer to Open the Heart

Dear Holy One,
I feel disconnected from my heart.

I can no longer let love in.
In spite of my endless mental commands,
love is barred from entering into its chambers.

My heart has protected itself
from the presence of love in my life
because it is so scarred and scared.

Please help me loosen the bolts around it
so that I may offer myself the permission
to be vulnerable enough
to love.

As long as I remain anchored to my soul,
it will always be safe to be loved.
I accept my heart as it is now,
trusting in my healing intentions
to smooth all resistance.
And so it is.
Amen.

Visualization

See a sheer, blackened mist of fear surrounding your heart. To create the courage to jump into the unknown, envision a bright red light emanating from the center of your heart. Breathe that red light into life as you let it grow and generate warmth until the black mist begins to dissipate. Your heart beats stronger now, in strength, in faith, and in love. You are grateful for the change, and you can bask in this heart revival for as long as you desire. No matter what occurs in your external world, the beat of love within you will always be there to catch you. Always.

Affirmations

I trust my heart to regain its wholeness.
My heart is powered by the love I generate.
My heart feels honored by my actions.
I love you, dear heart.

MEDITATION VIII:
Enhancing Energy

My energy is plummeting.
I need to ignite my life force.
I follow my breath into the ceaseless,
celestial meadow of spirit
to invigorate and restore my being.
Vitality blooms in my mind
and permeates my physical body
with its rejuvenating mist.
Each in-breath increases my vital energy.

Prayer to Find
A Spiritual Path

Dear Wisdom Keeper,
speak through the chimes of my intuition
to guide me to teachers, books, and experiences
that will resonate with my heart and spirit.
May I find a path that will lead me to
meet the Divine abiding in me.

May the resonance of your Truth
ring with unmistakable joy
as I recognize my way home.

I release unto you the curriculum
of my spiritual evolution toward becoming
a happier and more wholesome human being.

May I not be blinded by the glare of gurus,
instead allowing your magnetic guidance
to pull me to the Truth
that will restore my soul.

VISUALIZATION

Close your eyes and enter into your internal landscape by taking a few deep breaths and releasing them. You find yourself in an ancient Greek temple, surrounded by ten columns that form an open, rectangular room. The air is ancient and the presence of old wisdom is palpable. You sit in cross-legged position as the very center of the main room and place your hands on your lap, palms facing the skies to receive. Slow down yur mind by focusing on the beat of your heart, matching the beat of the Universe. In the silence of your mind, say:

"Dear Divine Keeper,
I am ready for the next step in my spiritual growth.
I desire to advance towards you, dear God.
How would you have me discover you?
How can I get to know you?
I desire to know the Truth and only the Truth.
I surrender the care of my soul
onto you in this moment.
I truly love you.
And so it is.
Amen."

AFFIRMATIONS

Truth belongs to the humble heart.
Knowing that I know nothing, I will to know Truth.
My soul is the caretaker of Truth.
I walk into the presence of Truth when I surrender my fears.

Prayer to Transform Mistakes

Dear Harvester of Wisdom,
I see that I have committed an error
that could have been avoided
and I feel the onset of guilt.

There is a thread
of potential discernment
running through every mortal experience
that can serve the emancipation of Love.

Please bless my inner vision to
behold the lesson of this experience.

May I dismiss the pride in my mind
so that my heart can feel full.

Help me flip my guilt
so that I may be enriched
by the wisdom contained in my error.
Amen.

VISUALIZATION

See a simple, rectangular altar in front of you. It is a holy place upon which you now place your regret over a recent mistake, to be transformed and forgiven into love. Surrender your error to the altar of the Divine, knowing it will be transmuted into wisdom and understanding. From that misstep, you will receive a fresh perspective on life and a deeper layer of wisdom. What do you need to learn from this? What is the gem of wisdom awaiting to be accepted? Welcome your higher self to guide you to that sacred understanding. Your errors are great conduits of wisdom and power if you open your heart to the sacred knowledge preciously held in your errors.

AFFIRMATIONS

I place my misstep in the care of love.
I am willing to take responsibility for my part in any problem.
I invite wisdom to transform my guilt.

Prayer for A Sacred Calling

I feel the impulse of my soul
amplifying with each beat of my heart.
There is nothing else I would rather pursue
with the years of my life.

I bow before you, dear spirit of creation,
and dedicate my light, my emotional work,
my sweat and tears to the birth of your creations
through my mortal means.

I pledge my devotion
to the highest good of humanity
in my creative and material endeavors.

May my mind be filled with grace,
and sustain what my spirit and body need
to reach the altitude of divine will.
I am now a devotee of my soul
as a messenger of your peace.
This life, I humbly give you.
Amen.

BENEDICTION

Together, we call on the highest wisdom
to infiltrate our minds and our hearts.
Bless us, dear God, with revelations
that show us the way to our soul-given function:
the fulfillment of love in this world.
We forgive ourselves for all our past detours,
and we are reborn in this holy instant.
We let our hearts open wide to engulf
and heal the ailments of our mind.
Pain, mistakes, heartbreaks, and shattered dreams
are always working for our highest good.
We follow the way appointed to us
by bowing to the light shining in all hearts.
May we revere our walk through life
on the way home to our undisturbed peace
and love everlasting.

ACKNOWLEDGMENTS

Thank you to my great-grandparents Marceau and Miralda for raising me.

Thank you Tata Marcette for always being the presence of love for me.

Thank you to my daughters Alissa and Shiloh for supporting their mother through our crazy lives.

Thank you Marianne Williamson for inspiring me to play big and deliver my message with love.

Thank you Judy Whitson for being an extraordinary presence of love.

Thank you D. Patrick Miller for believing in me before the world could.

Thank you, sweet fragrance of the Divine that is the light running throughout this book.

May prayer continue to
illuminate your spirit.